Third
Worst
Joke Book

Dumb Jokes for Kids
By Steve Burt

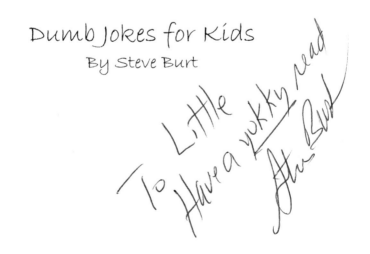

Third Worst Joke Book

Dumb Jokes for Kids

By Steve Burt

ISBN-13: 978-1539413578
ISBN-10: 1539413578

Steven E. Burt
The Villages, FL 32162
352 391-8293

For Gracie and Ben Thomas
who love dumb jokes

Third Worst Joke Book

 1. Why did Mozart kill all his chickens?
Because when he asked them who the best composer was, they'd all say, "Bach bach bach."

2. Knock knock.
Who's there?
Dwayne.
Dwayne who?

Dwayne the bathtub fast, I'm dwowning.

3. What's orange and sounds like a parrot?
A carrot.

Dumb Jokes for Kids

4. Why do vampires believe everything you tell them?
Because they're suckers.

5. What would bears be without bees?
Ears! (B+ ears)

6. Why did the skeleton go to the barbeque?
Because he wanted some spare ribs.

7. What color is a burp?
Burple.

BU-URRRPP!!!

8. What did the pirate say on
his 80th birthday?
Aye, matey.

9. Why does a moon rock
taste better than an earth
rock?
It's a little meteor.

Dumb Jokes for Kids

10. What happened when the butcher backed into his meat grinder?

He got a little behind in his work.

11. A friend of mine died recently after drinking a gallon of varnish.

It was a horrible end, but a lovely finish.

12. What's green and sings?

Elvis Parsley.

13. What does a clock do when it's hungry?

It goes back four seconds.

14. How do snails fight?

They slug it out.

15. Knock knock.

Who's there?

Little old lady.

Little old lady who?

I didn't know you could yodel.

Dumb Jokes for Kids

16. What did the policeman
say to his belly button?
You're under a vest.

17. What kind of pictures do
turtles take?
Shellfies.

18. How do you make a
bandstand?
Take away their chairs.

19. What should you do when you're attacked by a gang of carnival performers?
Go for the jugular.

20. Why was the worker fired from his job at the calendar factory?
He took a day off.

21. What do cats eat for breakfast?
Mice Krispies.

Dumb Jokes for Kids

22. How can you buy 4 suits
for a dollar?
Buy a deck of
cards.

23. What did the left ear say
to the right ear?
Between us, we have brains.

24. What's smaller than an
ant's mouth?

An ant's dinner.

25. How do you fix
a broken tuba?
With a tuba glue.

26. Is there a hole in your shoe?

No.

Then how'd you get your foot in it?

27. Why didn't the sun go to college?

Because he already had thousands of degrees.

28. A magician went driving down a road and turned into a driveway.

Dumb Jokes for Kids

29. How does a bear test its bath water?
With its bear (bare) feet.

30. What's the stupidest animal in the jungle?
The polar bear.

31. Why did the cookie cry?
His mother was a wafer so long.

32. What grows up while growing down?

A goose. (Down is another word for goose feathers.)

33. Did you hear about the bear that was hit by an 18-wheeler and splattered all over the place?
It was a grizzly accident.

34. Why isn't gambling allowed in Africa?
Too many cheetahs.

Dumb Jokes for Kids

35. What kind of music do mummies listen to?
Wrap music.

36. Have you heard the joke about the butter?
I can't tell you because you will spread it.

37. What do you call an annoying vampire?
A pain in the neck.

38. How do electric eels taste?

Shocking.

39. Why couldn't Dracula's wife sleep?
Because of his coffin.

40. What do you do with a sick boat?

Take it to the doc.

Dumb Jokes for Kids

41. What's the best way to carve wood?
Whittle by whittle.

42. Why are barns so noisy?
The cows have horns.

43. Why did the pig leave the party early?

Everyone thought he was a boar.

44. What do you call a
penguin in the desert?
Lost.

45. What did the grape do
when the elephant sat on it?
It let out a
little wine.

46. What is fastest, hot or
cold?
Hot, you can catch a cold.

Dumb Jokes for Kids

47. Where did the spaghetti go to dance? The meat ball.

48. If your nose runs and your feet smell, are you built upside down?

49. A toothless termite walks into a bar and asks, "Is the bar tender here?"

50. What goes "ha, ha, plop"? Someone laughing their head off.

Third Worst Joke Book

51. What do you call it when a dinosaur crashes his car?

Tyrannosaurus wrecks.

52. What goes boo-hoo, splat? Someone crying their eyes out.

53. Why don't clams and oysters donate to charity? They're shellfish.

Dumb Jokes for Kids

54. Why did the balloon burst?
Because it saw the
lollypop.

55. Why did the boy eat his homework?
The teacher said it
was a piece of cake.

56. What kind of flowers are on your face?
Tulips.

57. Did you hear about the kidnapping at school?
It's ok, he woke up.

58. What has four legs but can't run?
A table.

59. What invention was more important than the first telephone?
The second one.

60. Why couldn't the chicken find her eggs?
Because she mislaid them.

Dumb Jokes for Kids

61. How does the Man in the Moon cut his hair?
Eclipse it.

62. What did the ocean say to the pirate?
Nothing, it just waved.

63. Where does Frosty keep his cash?
In the snow banks.

64. What do clouds wear under their shorts?
Thunderpants.

65. Why did the guy sell his vacuum?
All it was doing
was collecting dust.

66. What do you call a fish with two knees?
A tunee fish.

67. Why are ghosts banned from liquor stores?
They steal all the boos.

68. Why do gorillas have big nostrils?
Because gorillas
have big fingers.

69. Did you hear the one about the three holes in the ground filled with water? No? Well, well, well.

70. Why shouldn't you go outside if it's raining cats and dogs? Because you might step in a poodle!

71. How many words are in The English Dictionary? Three.

Third Worst Joke Book

72. Why does Humpty
Dumpty love autumn?
He had a great fall.

73. What are two things you
can't have for lunch?
Breakfast and dinner.

74. Why did the computer
need glasses?
To fix his web sight.

75. What's black and white
and red all over?
A newspaper.

Dumb Jokes for Kids

76. Why did the pirate go to the Caribbean?
For some arr and arr.
(R&R is short for Rest and Relaxation)

77. What do calendars eat?
Dates.

78. Did you hear the story about the really messy bed?
Of course not, it hasn't been made up yet.

79. What does a spy do when he gets cold?
He goes undercover.

Third Worst Joke Book

80. Why does lightning shock people?
Because it doesn't know how to conduct itself.

81. A farmer had 199 cows in his pasture, but when he rounded them up,
he had 200.

82. What do bumblebees put in the bathtub first?
Their bee-hinds.

83. What do computers snack on?
Microchips.

Dumb Jokes for Kids

84. Did you hear the story about the unsharpened pencil?
There's really no point to it.

85. Two fish are in a tank. One turns to the other and says, "how do you drive this thing?"

86. I never wanted to believe that my Dad was stealing from his job as a road worker.

 But when I got home, all the signs were there.

87. Why did the astronomer dump beef on his head?
He wanted a meatier shower.

88. Did you hear about the 2 guys who stole a calendar?
They each got 6 months.

89. I had a dream I was a muffler and I woke up exhausted.

90. Knock, knock.
Who's there?
Atch.
Atch who?
I didn't know you had a cold!

Dumb Jokes for Kids

91. What happened when the red ship and the blue ship collided?
The crew was marooned.

92. I hated my job as an origami teacher. Too much paperwork.

93. Two nuns are driving down the road when Dracula jumps out.
"Quick," says the first, "show him your cross".
The other leans out the window and yells, "Get out of the road, you jerk!"

Third Worst Joke Book

94. What did the mountain climber name his son?
Cliff.

95. I wondered why the Frisbee kept getting bigger, and then it hit me.

96. A man walks into a library and says to the librarian:
"Fish and chips, please."
The librarian says, "Beg your pardon, but this is a library."
So the man says, "Oh, sorry," and whispers, "Fish and chips, please."

Dumb Jokes for Kids

97. Somebody said you sounded like an owl. Who?

98. Why didn't the skeleton attack the trick-or-treater? It didn't have the guts.

99. Did you hear about the guy who invented Lifesavers? They say he made a mint.

Third Worst Joke Book

100. When I asked Dad to make me a sandwich, he waved his hand over my head and said, "Poof, you're a sandwich!

101. How can you tell if an ant is a male or a female? They're all females, otherwise they'd be uncles.

102. Why is milk the world's fastest liquid? It's pasteurized before you even see it.

Dumb Jokes for Kids

 103. What's Forrest Gump's password?
1forrest1

104. What's ET short for?
Because he's only got little legs.

105. Where can you get chicken broth in bulk?
The stock market.

106. What is Beethoven's favorite fruit?
A ba-na-na-na.

107. What do you call an Argentinian with a rubber toe?
Roberto

108. What do you call a man with no nose and no body?
Nobody nose.

109. What do you call a man with no arms and no legs lying in front of your door?
Matt.

110. How does frogs kill themselves?
They Kermit suicide.

111. I cut my finger chopping cheese, but I may have grater problems.

112. My cat was just sick on the carpet. I don't think it's feline well.

Third Worst Joke Book

113. Did you hear about the guy who gave away all his dead batteries?
They were free of charge.

114. I needed a password eight characters long so I picked Snow White and the Seven Dwarfs.

115. What did the man who feared elevators do?
He took steps to avoid them.

Dumb Jokes for Kids

116. What's the advantage of living in Switzerland?
Their flag is a big plus.

117. Why did the octopus beat the shark in a fight?
Because it was well armed.

118. Why did the guy delete his German friends' phone numbers on his cell phone?
So it would be Hans free.

119. Last night Dad and I watched three DVDs back to back. Luckily I was the one facing the TV.

120. What did daddy spider say to baby spider?
You spend too much time on the web.

121. What do you call a group of killer whales playing instruments?
An Orca-stra.

Dumb Jokes for Kids

122. I watched a
documentary
about beavers.

Best dam program ever.

123. What happened when the
Energizer Bunny
was arrested?

He was charged with battery.

124. A Sandwich walks into
a bar.

The bartender says "Sorry,
we don't serve food here."

Third Worst Joke Book

125. The man said, "Doctor,
I've broken my arm in
several places." So the doctor
said, "Well, don't go to those
places."

126. Have you heard about
America' most popular new
broom?
It's sweeping the
nation.

127. Did you hear about the
kid reading a book on the
History of Glue?
He couldn't put it down.

Dumb Jokes for Kids

128. What did the
daddy tomato
yell to the baby
tomato?
Catch up.

129. What did baby corn say
to mama corn?
Where's popcorn?

130. What did the father
buffalo say to his little boy
buffalo when he dropped him
off at school?
Bison.

Third Worst Joke Book

131. What did the
duck say when it
walked into the
drugstore?
Give me some chap-stick and
put it on my bill.

132. Why did the scarecrow
win an award?
He was
outstanding in his field.

133. Why did the girl smear
peanut butter on the road?
To go with the
traffic jam.

Dumb Jokes for Kids

134. Why does a chicken coop only have two doors? Because if it had four doors it would be a chicken sedan. (A coupe is a 2-door car, a sedan is a 4-door car.)

135. Why don't seagulls fly over the bay? Because then they'd be bay-gulls!

136. What did the cop discover when he found two peanuts on the street? One was a salted.

137. What's the difference between an African elephant and an Indian elephant?

About 5000 miles.

138. What do you call rapper Jay-Z when he's sleeping?
Jay Zzzzzzzzz.

139. Why are skeletons so calm?
Nothing gets
under their skin.

Dumb Jokes for Kids

140. Why don't skeletons ever go trick or treating? They have no body to go with.

141. Why do scuba divers fall backwards into the water?

 Because if they fell forwards they'd still be in the boat.

142. What kind of music does the band Cell-O-Phone sing?
They mostly wrap.

143. What kind of magic do cows believe in?
MOODOO.

144. Why does it take longer to get from 1st to 2nd base than it does to get from 2nd to 3rd?
There's a shortstop in between.

145. How do you know when you are going to drown in milk?
When it's past your eyes!

Dumb Jokes for Kids

146. What did Snow White
say when she came out of the
photo booth?
Someday my prints will
come.

147. Why did the cyclops
close his school?
Because he only had one
pupil.

148. I'm trying to decide
whether I want an open-
casket funeral.
Remains to be
seen.

Third Worst Joke Book

149. What do you call a
computer that sings?
Adell.

150. What do you call a can
opener that doesn't work?
A can't opener!

151. What sound does a nut
make when it sneezes?
Cashew.

152. Why don't dinosaurs
talk?
Because they're
dead.

Dumb Jokes for Kids

153. I've got a knock-knock joke. You start.
Knock-knock.
Who's there?
. . .

154. Why did the cannibals refuse to eat the clowns?
They tasted
funny.

155. Why does Piglet smell?
Because he plays with Pooh
all day.

If you enjoyed Steve Burt's ***Third Worst Joke Book***, you'll love ***First*** and ***Second Worst Joke Books*** in his ***Dumb Jokes for Kids*** series. Available in print or e-book.

Steve writes other good stuff, too. His ***FreeKs*** series, featuring paranormal teen detectives, has won 4 Mom's Choice Awards.

And his ghost story collections (***Stories to Chill the Heart series***) won the Bram Stoker Award for Young Readers (the genre's top prize). They can be found on Amazon or at the author's website.
www.SteveBurtBooks.com